VAN GOGH ARTWORK
DESK CALENDAR 2025

All rights reserved. No part of this book may be reproduced or transmitted in any form or by any means, including but not limited to information storage and retrieval systems, electronic, mechanical, photocopy, recording, etc. without written permission from the copyright holder.
The 12 images used in this desk calendar book are paintings by Vincent Van Gogh and are in the Public Domain. © Llama Bird Press All Rights Reserved 2025

Almond Blossoms, 1890 by Vincent Van Gogh

JANUARY | 2025

SUNDAY	MONDAY	TUESDAY	WEDNESDAY	THURSDAY	FRIDAY	SATURDAY
			1 New Year's Day	2	3	4
5	6	7	8	9	10	11
12	13	14	15	16	17	18
19	20 Martin Luther King Jr. Day	21	22	23	24	25
26	27	28	29 Chinese New Year	30	31	

GOALS

NOTES

TO DO LIST

Wheatfield with Crows, 1890 by Vincent Van Gogh

February | 2025

GOALS

NOTES

TO DO LIST

SUNDAY	MONDAY	TUESDAY	WEDNESDAY	THURSDAY	FRIDAY	SATURDAY
						1
2	3	4	5	6	7	8
9	10	11	12	13	14 *Valentine's Day*	15
16	17 *President's Day*	18	19	20	21	22
23	24	25	26	27	28	

The Starry Night, 1889 by Vincent Van Gogh

MARCH | 2025

SUNDAY	MONDAY	TUESDAY	WEDNESDAY	THURSDAY	FRIDAY	SATURDAY
						1
2	3	4	5 Ash Wednesday	6	7	8
9	10	11	12	13	14	15
16	17 St. Patrick's Day	18	19	20	21	22
23	24	25	26	27	28	29
30	31					

GOALS

NOTES

TO DO LIST

WHEATFIELD WITH CYPRESSES, 1889 BY VINCENT VAN GOGH

APRIL | 2025

SUNDAY	MONDAY	TUESDAY	WEDNESDAY	THURSDAY	FRIDAY	SATURDAY
		1 April Fool's Day	2	3	4	5
6	7	8	9	10	11	12
13 Passover	14	15	16	17	18	19
20 Easter	21	22 Earth Day	23	24	25	26
27	28	29	30			

GOALS

NOTES

TO DO LIST

THE SOWER, 1888 BY VINCENT VAN GOGH

MAY | 2025

SUNDAY	MONDAY	TUESDAY	WEDNESDAY	THURSDAY	FRIDAY	SATURDAY
				1	2	3
4	5 Cinco de Mayo	6	7	8	9	10
11 Mother's Day	12	13	14	15	16	17
18	19	20	21	22	23	24
25	26 Memorial Day	27	28	29	30	31

GOALS

NOTES

TO DO LIST

THE NIGHT CAFE, 1888 BY VINCENT VAN GOGH

June | 2025

SUNDAY	MONDAY	TUESDAY	WEDNESDAY	THURSDAY	FRIDAY	SATURDAY
1	2	3	4	5	6	7
8 **Pentecost**	9	10	11	12	13	14 **Flag Day**
15 **Father's Day**	16	17	18	19 **Juneteenth**	20	21 **June Solstice**
22	23	24	25	26	27	28
29	30					

GOALS

NOTES

TO DO LIST

Noon Rest At Work, 1890 by Vincent Van Gogh

JULY | 2025

SUNDAY	MONDAY	TUESDAY	WEDNESDAY	THURSDAY	FRIDAY	SATURDAY
		1	2	3	4 — Independence Day	5
6	7	8	9	10	11	12
13	14	15	16	17	18	19
20	21	22	23	24	25	26
27	28	29	30	31		

GOALS

NOTES

TO DO LIST

Starry Night Over The Rhone, 1888 by Vincent Van Gogh

August | 2025

SUNDAY	MONDAY	TUESDAY	WEDNESDAY	THURSDAY	FRIDAY	SATURDAY
					1	2
3	4	5	6	7	8	9
10	11	12	13	14	15	16
17	18	19	20	21	22	23
24	25	26	27	28	29	30
31						

GOALS

NOTES

TO DO LIST

THE RED VINEYARD AT ARLES, 1888 BY VINCENT VAN GOGH

September | 2025

GOALS

NOTES

TO DO LIST

SUNDAY	MONDAY	TUESDAY	WEDNESDAY	THURSDAY	FRIDAY	SATURDAY
	1 Labor Day	2	3	4	5	6
7 Grandparents Day	8	9	10	11	12	13
14	15	16	17	18	19	20
21	22	23 Rosh Hashanah	24	25	26	27
28	29	30				

STILL LIFE WITH BIBLE, 1885 BY VINCENT VAN GOGH

October | 2025

SUNDAY	MONDAY	TUESDAY	WEDNESDAY	THURSDAY	FRIDAY	SATURDAY
			1	2	3	4
5	6	7	8	9	10	11
12	13	14	15	16	17	18
19	20	21	22	23	24	25
26	27	28	29	30	31 Halloween	

GOALS

NOTES

TO DO LIST

The Potato Eaters, 1885 by Vincent Van Gogh

November | 2025

GOALS							
	SUNDAY	MONDAY	TUESDAY	WEDNESDAY	THURSDAY	FRIDAY	SATURDAY
				1	2	3	4
	5	6	7	8	9	10	11 Veterans Day
NOTES	12	13	14	15	16	17	18
	19	20	21	22	23	24	25
TO DO LIST	26	27 Thanksgiving	28	29	30	31	

IRISES, 1889 BY VINCENT VAN GOGH

December | 2025

SUNDAY	MONDAY	TUESDAY	WEDNESDAY	THURSDAY	FRIDAY	SATURDAY
	1	2	3	4	5	6
7	8	9	10	11	12	13
14 Hanukkah begins	15	16	17	18	19	20
21 December Solstice	22	23	24 Christmas Eve	25 Christmas Day	26 Kwanzaa begins	27
28	29	30	31 New Year's Eve			

GOALS

NOTES

TO DO LIST

© Llama Bird
PRESS

www.ingramcontent.com/pod-product-compliance
Lightning Source LLC
Chambersburg PA
CBHW041644070526

44585CB00005B/128